LET'S LEARN ABOUT
COMPUTER SCIENCE

ALGORITHMS

Jeff Mapua

Enslow Publishing
101 W. 23rd Street
Suite 240
New York, NY 10011
USA

enslow.com

WORDS TO KNOW

algorithm A step-by-step way to solve a problem.

conditional When something is true only if something else is true.

function A set of directions used by a computer.

problem Something that needs to be worked out or solved.

repeat To do something more than once.

sequence To place things in order; things that are placed in order.

solution The answer to a problem.

task A job.

CONTENTS

In hopscotch,
you hop on one
square at a time.

Step-by-Step

How do you follow directions? Your mom tells you to brush your teeth. Do you put toothpaste on your toothbrush before you rinse? **Tasks** are done one step at a time.

Fast Fact

It is easier to do one thing at a time than many things at once.

Packing your backpack is one step you take when you get ready for school.

Problems

A **problem** can be many things. Getting ready for school is one kind of problem. Finding a lost book is another problem.

FAST FACT

The most powerful computers today can work like a human brain!

When something is broken, you can find a way to fix it.

Solutions

Problems can be fixed. The way to fix a problem is called a **solution**. Once you solve a problem, you can use the same solution to fix it again.

**A recipe has steps that you follow in order.
An algorithm is like a recipe.**

Algorithms

An **algorithm** is a kind of solution. It is a step-by-step way to solve a problem. Brushing your teeth follows an algorithm. Put the toothpaste on the toothbrush. Then brush your teeth. Then rinse.

Fast Fact

Computers follow algorithms to complete large tasks.

When you solve a
math problem, you use
an algorithm.

Helpful Algorithms

Algorithms are used in many ways. They can be used with math problems. Can you find the sum of ten plus ten? Add the ones place first. Next add the tens place. You just used an algorithm!

When you ask a
computer to do
something, it uses
an algorithm to
complete the task.

Computers and Algorithms

Computers use algorithms to do tasks. This means they follow directions to complete a **function**. A function is what we want the computer to do. This could be spell check, search, or add numbers.

Fast Fact

A computer will always follow an algorithm the same way.

**Repetition is doing
something over
and over again.**

Repetition

Algorithm directions have to be very clear. **Repeating** is one kind of direction. Computers can do the same thing five, ten, or a hundred times!

FAST FACT

In computer programming, a "repeat" direction can be called a loop.

Sequence is important. You have to be able to walk before you can run.

Sequencing

Computer algorithms must follow a special order. This is called **sequencing**. Think about getting ready for the day. First you put on your shoes. Then you walk out the door.

Fast Fact

Breaking the order of a sequence can make a computer fail.

**You cross the street only
if the traffic light is green.**

Conditional Steps

A computer can do tasks when something is true. This is known as **conditional** steps. You walk outside only if your shoes are on. If they are not on, you do not go outside.

Activity
Fun with Algorithms

MATERIALS
notebook
pencil

Do you want to write your own algorithms? Here are some ways to start:

Think about your day. What problems have you solved? Is there something you do every day?

Do you make your breakfast?

Do you pack up your backpack?

Write down how you carry out your task or solve a problem. Try to make instructions so someone else could do the same thing. Remember to be very clear so someone else can understand what you mean. Be as specific as possible.

LEARN MORE

Books

Hoena, Blake. *Algorithms: Solve A Problem!* North Mankato, MN: Cantata Learning, 2018.

Labrecque, Ellen. *Ada Lovelace and Computer Algorithms*. North Mankato, MN: Cherry Lake, 2017.

Lyons, Heather, and Elizabeth Tweedale. *Coding, Bugs, and Fixes*. Minneapolis, MN: Lerner, 2016.

Websites

Khan Academy

www.khanacademy.org / computing / computer-science / algorithms
Learn the basics of algorithms with fun activities for the family.

Learning Code for Kids

learningcodeforkids.com / angry-birds-online
Play a fun game to learn about repetition, conditionals, and simple algorithms.

INDEX

Published in 2019 by Enslow Publishing, LLC.
101 W. 23rd Street, Suite 240, New York, NY 10011

Library of Congress Cataloging-in-Publication Data

Names: Mapua, Jeff, author.
Title: Algorithms / Jeff Mapua.
Description: New York : Enslow Publishing, LLC., 2019. | Series: Let's learn about computer science | Audience: K to grade 4.
Identifiers: LCCN 2018001426| ISBN 9781978501775 (library bound) | ISBN 9781978502215 (pbk.) | ISBN 9781978502222 (6 pack)
Subjects: LCSH: Computer algorithms—Juvenile literature. | File organization (Computer science)—Juvenile literature. | Computer programming—Juvenile literature.
Classification: LCC QA76.9.A43 M3868 2019 | DDC 005.74/1—dc23

LC record available at https://lccn.loc.gov/2018001426

Printed in the United States of America

To Our Readers: We have done our best to make sure all website addresses in this book were active and appropriate when we went to press. However, the author and the publisher have no control over and assume no liability for the material available on those websites or on any websites they may link to. Any comments or suggestions can be sent by e-mail to customerservice@enslow.com.

Photos Credits: Cover, p. 1 Vintage Tone/Shutterstock.com; pp. 2, 3, 24 Best-Backgrounds/Shutterstock.com; p. 4 Golden Pixels LLC/Shutterstock.com; p. 6 kryzhov/Shutterstock.com; p. 8 noprati somchit/Shutterstock.com; p. 10 2xSamara.com/Shutterstock.com; p. 12 GagliardiImages/Shutterstock.com; p. 14 Sergey Maksienko/Shutterstock.com; p. 16 Arkom Suvarnasiri/Shutterstock.com; p. 18 Serega K Photo and Video/Shutterstock.com; p. 20 Dmitri Ma/Shutterstock.com; p. 22 Freebird7977/Shutterstock.com; interior design elements (laptop) ArthurStock/ Shutterstock.com, (flat screen computer) Aleksandrs Bondars/ Shutterstock.com.